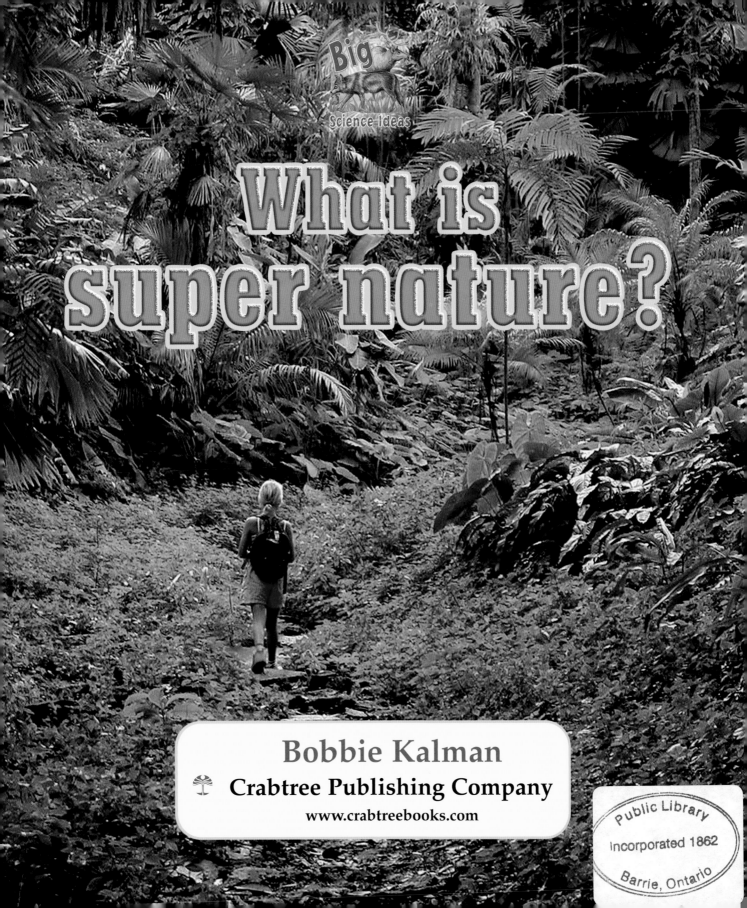

Big
Science Ideas

What is super nature?

Bobbie Kalman

Crabtree Publishing Company

www.crabtreebooks.com

What is super nature?

No matter where we live, we need **nature**. Nature is all the things on Earth, such as air, water, plants, animals, rocks, and other materials, that have not been made by people. **Super nature** is about the amazing things that plants and animals can do that people wish they could do. For example, no machine can make oxygen from sunlight the way plants can, and plants do it for free! The more we learn about the super powers of nature, the cleaner and safer our world will be.

*We have learned to catch the sun's energy with **solar panels** like these. To make solar panels, we need electricity and many kinds of materials that cost money. Leaves catch sunlight for free.*

Nature friendly

What can we learn from nature to
live in ways that do not hurt the Earth?
We can learn these important things:

- nature runs on sunlight
- nature recycles everything
- nature does not waste anything
- nature is always changing
- every part of nature is important

We recycle everything!

Super sunlight

Plants, animals, and people are **living things**. All living things need **energy**. Energy is the power that living things need to breathe, grow, move, and stay alive. Plants use the sun's energy to make their own food. Making food from sunlight is called **photosynthesis**. Photosynthesis means "putting together with light." Plants put water and a part of air called **carbon dioxide** together with sunlight to make food. Without sunlight, nothing could live on Earth. Sunlight runs nature, and it does it for free.

*Leaves contain **chlorophyll**, a green **pigment**, or natural color. Chlorophyll catches sunlight for photosynthesis.*

*When leaves make food, they also make **oxygen**. Oxygen is the part of air that people and animals need to breathe.*

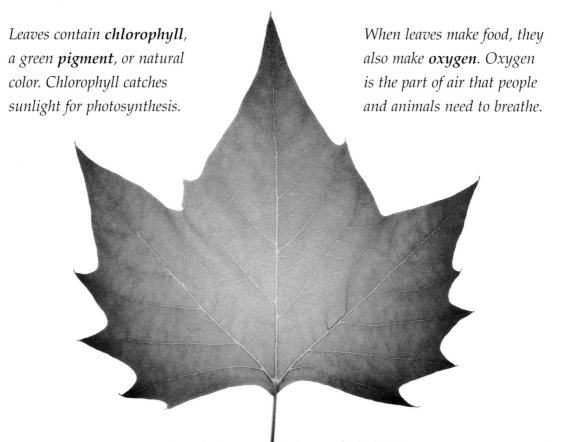

Nature runs on sunlight

Sunlight provides Earth with heat and light. It also gives us colors. You can see the sun's colors in this rainbow. They are: red, orange, yellow, green, blue, indigo (dark blue), and violet (purple).

Super food energy

The energy of the sun is passed along in food. It is passed from living thing to living thing. Plants use the sun's energy to make food. The sun's energy is then stored in the plants. People and animals cannot make food, but they need to eat food to get energy. Some animals, called **herbivores**, eat mainly plant foods. They get the energy of the sun from the plants they eat. Some animals, called **carnivores**, eat herbivores. Carnivores get the energy of the sun from the herbivores, who get their energy from plants. The energy of the sun is passed along in **food chains**.

The energy of the sun is passed along from the plant to the rabbit and to the fox in this food chain.

sun

*fox
(carnivore)*

*rabbit
(herbivore)*

plants

Nature does not waste

When living things die, they still have energy and **nutrients** in their bodies. The energy and nutrients are used by other living things. Living things that eat dead things help clean the Earth, and they pass along energy and nutrients. Some of "nature's cleaners" put the nutrients back into the soil to help new plants grow. The food chain then starts again with the new plants. Nature does not waste energy or nutrients.

This eagle has found a dead fox to eat. It will eat some of it and leave the rest for other animals to finish.

Maggots and earthworms take the energy in dead things and pass it back into the Earth.

maggots

earthworm

bacteria

The energy of dead things goes back into the soil. New plants grow in the soil.

fungi

Bacteria and fungi break down dead things even more.

Is my food super natural?

In nature, animals eat the foods that give them the nutrients they need. In the past, people also ate foods that were natural and which gave them the nutrients they needed. Now, we eat a lot of foods that have unhealthy things added to them. If we eat too many of these foods, they can make us sick.

Many of the foods we eat contain too much fat, sugar, salt, and other things that do not keep us healthy. We can be super natural by eating foods that are good for our bodies.

10

Eating fresh foods gives our bodies the energy they need. Eating a rainbow of foods every day is a healthy way to eat. Fruits and vegetables of each color contain different nutrients that help our bodies in different ways.

Vegetable gardens give us super foods. If you do not have one, you can ask your parents to buy foods that are grown close to your home.

Organic food comes from plants that are grown without **pesticides** and from animals that eat natural foods, such as pesticide-free grass.

11

Super bees

Did you know that one-third of all the food you eat depends on **pollinators**? Pollinators are animals that spread **pollen** from one plant to another. Pollen is a yellow powder found in the middle of flowers. The spreading of pollen from flower to flower is called **pollination**. After a flower is pollinated, the plant can make fruit and seeds. Pollinators make plants healthier so they can make a lot of food. There are thousands of kinds of pollinators, but honeybees are the most important.

pollen sac

pollen

*When a bee lands on a flower, it collects pollen in its **pollen sacs**. Some of the pollen rubs off on the next flower it visits. That next flower is then pollinated.*

What do bees pollinate?

Most kinds of fruits, vegetables, and some kinds of nuts come from plants that were pollinated by bees. Honeybees also make honey. Without bees, there would be no honey, many kinds of vegetables and fruits, or nuts such as almonds and cashews. Bees are super nature in action!

Bees in trouble

Bees are disappearing from many places. People are not sure why they are dying, but many feel that pesticides, **parasites**, and diseases may be to blame.

Helping bees

We can help bees by not using pesticides in our gardens, by planting flowers that bees like, by caring for nature, and by telling others how super bees are!

Animal healers

Did you know that many animals in the wild can heal themselves when they are sick? Some of our medicines have come from nature, too. Animals taught people which plants would help them feel better when they had pains, such as stomachaches or even serious illnesses.

Lemurs know which leaves to eat when they are not feeling well.

*Cats of all kinds, from pet cats to lions, eat grass when they feel sick. Cats cannot **digest** grass and will vomit it up, along with **poisons** and fur balls. Cats get fur balls when they lick their fur to clean themselves.*

The big ears of rabbits help trap sunshine.
Rabbits have oil in their ears that uses
sunshine to build vitamin D. This vitamin
helps make bones strong. When rabbits
wipe their ears with their paws and then
lick their paws, they put this important
vitamin into their mouths.

We need vitamin D, too, for our bones.
The best place to get vitamin D is outdoors in
sunshine. Make sure you wear some sunscreen!

Animals eat hibiscus plants to cure all
kinds of sicknesses. People drink hibiscus
tea for its many healing nutrients.

15

Super-strong silk!

Some spiders build webs, but all spiders spin silk. Some spin as many as six kinds! Spiders use the silk to escape from danger, build homes, and trap **prey**. Prey are the animals they hunt and eat. Web-weaving spiders catch prey in their sticky webs. They wrap the prey in silk and shoot a liquid into them that turns the insides of the prey to juice. The spiders then suck up the liquid and leave behind an empty shell.

Stronger than steel

Spider silk is very strong. It is also very stretchy and does not break, even in very hot or cold temperatures. Some spider silk is five times as strong as steel! Making steel **pollutes**, or dirties, air and water, but spiders do not pollute air or water while they spin silk. If people could learn how to produce spider silk, it could be used to make many things, including clothing and even new body parts for people!

spider drinking its prey

This spider is wrapping a bee in silk. It will then turn the insides of the bee into liquid.

17

Super travelers

Some animals **migrate**. To migrate is to move from one area to another and then back again. Some animals migrate to warm places to escape winter. Other animals migrate to lay eggs or have babies in other parts of the world. Migrating animals do not take ships or planes. They use their own energy to travel, and they **navigate**, or find their way, without maps.

Humpback whales migrate from the cold oceans near the North Pole to warm ocean waters to have their babies. The calves are born without much fat and would freeze in icy ocean water.

From north to south

The Arctic tern migrates farther than any other animal! In June and July, terns live in the Arctic, near the North Pole. They begin their long journeys south in August, to the other end of the Earth. By December, they reach the areas near the South Pole, where it is summer. When summer is over, the terns fly back home again to the Arctic.

Terns lay their eggs and raise their baby birds in the Arctic.

Terns fly almost all year long. They fly above oceans so they can find fish to eat on their journeys.

Super fliers

The ruby-throated hummingbird is a tiny bird that can really fly! It can fly at fast speeds, quickly change direction, and **hover**. To hover is to stay in one place in the air. Ruby-throated hummingbirds can fly up to 26 hours without eating any food! They fly over the Gulf of Mexico, which is a huge area of ocean. Before they migrate, the hummingbirds fatten up by eating insects and drinking a lot of **nectar**. They nearly double their body weight before they start their long journeys.

When hummingbirds hover, their wings seem to disappear!

There are no places to stop over an ocean, so these tiny birds have just enough energy to make their dangerous trip. Could you fly across an ocean like a hummingbird?

21

Super bodies

Some animals have special body parts that allow them to send long-distance messages, to find objects using sound, to make their own light, and to see colors that we cannot see. The pictures on these two pages show some of the super-natural things that animals can do!

*Some kinds of jellyfish can make light. Making light is called **bioluminescence**. The light scares away **predators** that might eat the jellyfish.*

*Elephants can hear **infrasound**, or low sounds that we cannot hear, and can pick up sounds in the air with their trunks. They stomp their feet to send messages through the ground, too. Other elephants can hear the "stomps" from as far away as 31 miles (50 km).*

Echolocation is a way of hearing and seeing with sound. Echolocation gives dolphins information about where to find food. Dolphins send out clicking sounds. From the echoes that come back, the dolphins learn the location of food and can "see" what kind of food it is.

A woodpecker uses great force to drill holes in trees. Its head and bill are not hurt by the force of the drilling!

*Bees and butterflies can see **ultraviolet** colors that we cannot see. Ultraviolet colors and patterns guide them to the flowers where they will find food.*

23

Super builders

Termites are **insects**. Some termites make huge homes called **mounds**. Termite mounds can be as tall as 30 feet (9 meters). These homes are even more amazing inside! Termites build mounds that always stay about the same temperature. The queen of the **colony**, or community, directs the building of the mound by giving off **scent**, or smell, messages. The workers build the mounds using mud and their **saliva**, or spit. The termites keep the mounds at the same temperature by opening and closing heating and cooling **vents** during the day and at night.

queen

vents →

Learning from termites

How could termites teach us about heating and air-conditioning our homes without using oil or electricity? The Eastgate Centre in Harare, Zimbabwe, is modeled after termite mounds. This large office building and shopping mall does not have regular air-conditioning or heating, yet it stays about the same temperature and uses one-tenth the energy that other buildings use. It uses the same kinds of heating and cooling vents as those found in termite mounds.

termite queen and workers

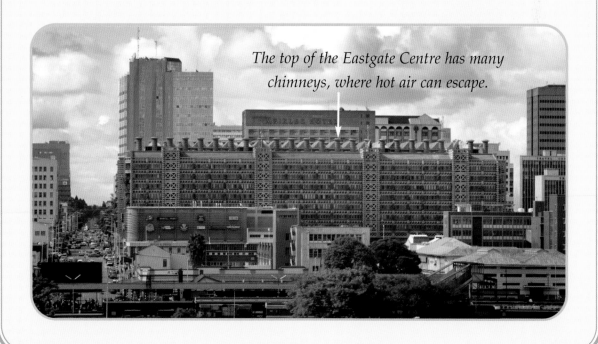

The top of the Eastgate Centre has many chimneys, where hot air can escape.

25

Super trees

Trees are super nature in action! Their leaves make food. Animals eat their bark, leaves, nuts, seeds, and fruits. Trees clean the air we breathe by taking carbon dioxide out of the air and putting oxygen back in. Trees are the **lungs** of the Earth! Our lungs are the body parts that breathe air.

Shade, water, homes

Trees cool the air, too. Their branches and leaves provide shade from the sun. Their roots store water and keep the soil moist. Trees are also home to birds, apes, monkeys, squirrels, and many other animals. How could our homes be built to do the things that trees can do?

Gibbons spend most of their time in trees. They sleep and find fruit to eat in trees.

27

I can be super natural!

We can copy nature and become more super natural. We can eat natural foods that are grown where we live. We can save energy by turning off lights, TV sets, and computers when we are not using them. We can walk, ride our bikes, or take buses. We can spend more time in nature and learn why it is so amazing! What things can you do to be more super natural?

I am super natural! Are you?

I ride my bike to school and when I visit my friends.

I can be a nature's cleaner by putting my leftover foods into a **compost** bin. Compost is broken down by worms and bacteria. It can later be used to make better soil. I can grow new plants in the soil.

compost bin

Compost contains energy and nutrients.

(left) I can spend more time in nature. I can look at plants and watch animals in action. I can learn how to be super natural by learning from super nature.

(right) I can recycle paper, plastic, and cans so they can be used to make new things. When I recycle, I cut down on waste.

29

Our super-natural Earth

Within us are all the super parts of nature, but we sometimes forget that we, too, are part of nature. The sun's energy is in the food we eat, the oxygen made by trees is in the air we breathe, and more than half of our bodies are made up of water. We do not think these things are valuable because they are free. We think the things that are important are the things we can buy, and we soon throw them away because we always want new things. We need to change the way we think. We need to be thankful to nature and protect it because we are nature, too!

Make one change

If everyone made just one change to help the Earth, the results would be huge! Here are some easy things you can do. Show Earth your love and start now!

Carry water in reusable drinking containers.

- Grow your own fruits and vegetables or buy foods that are grown close to home.
- Eat more real foods and have a meat-free day once a week. Cows create gases that are dangerous to the Earth and to people.
- Do not buy bottled water or other bottled drinks. Drink filtered tap water from a glass or a reusable drink container.
- Don't buy things that you do not need just because they are new. Start a second-hand club and trade your toys, books, and clothes. Other people's things will be "new" to you.
- When you are kind to the Earth, you are kind to yourself, too, because you are part of Earth.
- Get out into nature and really look at its beauty. Earth is your super-beautiful, super-natural home. You, too, can be super natural. You are nature!

(left) Create your own fashion style using your old clothes or second-hand clothes.

Trade books and toys with your friends.

Grow your own vegetables or buy them at a local market.

Glossary

Note: Some boldfaced words are defined where they appear in the book.

bioluminescence The glow of light made by some animals such as jellyfish and fireflies

chlorophyll A natural green color found in plants that allows them to make food

digest To break down food so that the body can use it for energy

echolocation An animal's ability to locate objects by sending out and receiving sounds

infrasound Sound that is too low to be heard by humans

insect A small animal with six legs

photosynthesis The way that green plants use sunlight to make food from air and water

nectar A sweet liquid in flowers

nutrient A substance that living things need to grow and stay healthy

parasite A creature that feeds off a living plant or animal's body

pesticide A chemical sprayed on plants to kill insects

poison A substance that is harmful to a living thing

vent An opening through which air or gas passes

Index